15

You Just Have To Laugh Publishing

First published in the USA in 2008
You Just Have to Laugh Publishing
Lenexa, Kansas U.S.A.
youjusthavetolaugh.com or naster.com
Printed in Korea by asianprinting.com

2 4 6 8 10 9 7 5 3 1

First Printing: 2008 August
Library of Congress Catalog Number:
2008930379
ISBN: 0966314581

Design by Nancy Loughlin and David Naster

CONTENTS

-Important words

People WANT to laugh at death

People NEED to laugh at death.

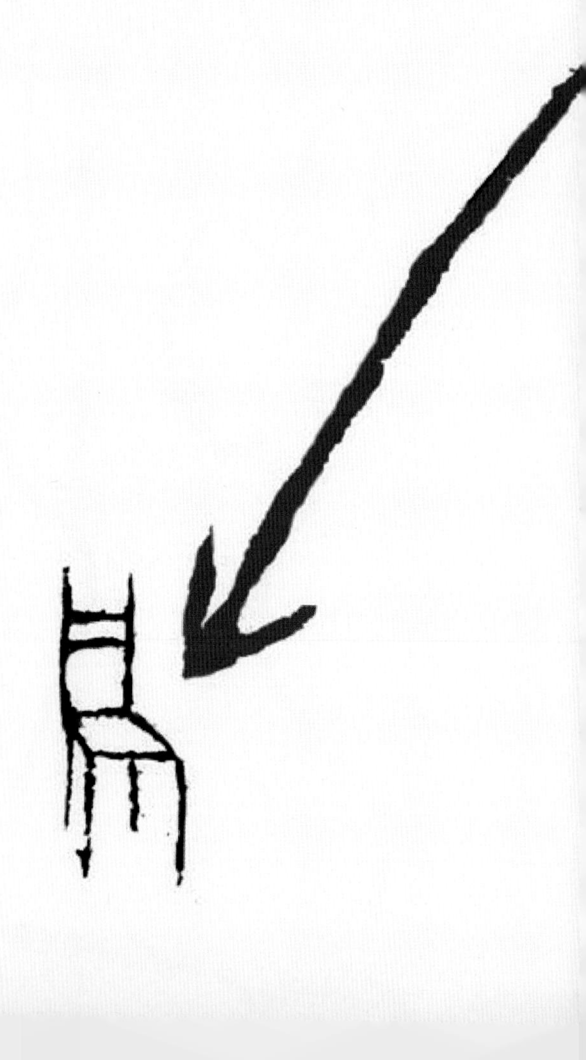

– Humor frees us from sadness and disarms fear.

Trappist Monks aren't saddened or frightened by death. They greet each other with, "Momento Mori" – remember you're dying. They keep in their thoughts that they're mortal. This daily reminder leads to a life of meaning – appreciating every precious second.

"It is with passion and reverence I offer you a new way of thinking – the possibility of finding humor in what scares us the most. You may not be ready to laugh at death. I understand. This guidebook is available when you are.

"Before I ever heard of a Trappist Monk I wouldn't have believed that death could be the meaning of life. I do now!"

"Momento Mori"
David

Thanks Elaine!

"The advice 'keep your sense of humor' may seem out of place in dealing with life-limiting illness and death. Our experience shows that even in the midst of great sorrow, laughter can be a welcome gift.

"There is a great deal of research proving the healing effects of laughing. There is no greater time we need to heal than when we are grieving.

"Time after time, we see a heavy heart made lighter when something funny happens. Humor helps everyone, from the family to the professional caregiver – release stress, cope with a difficult situation and confront our fears.

"Whether you are grieving or you just like to laugh, heal yourself by reading this book."

– Elaine McIntosh, President and CEO
Kansas City Hospice & Palliative Care

humor

Death

our biggest fear

Mortality –
I am going to die.

Abandonment –
I'll be completely alone

Unknown –
Where do I go after I die?

Humor

eliminates fear

Humor is the skill of thinking funny.

The thought of death suffocates living.

Thinking funny loosens death's noose on our psyche.

HUMOR

... is created from a set-up
followed by a punch line.

The set-up
is something to joke about.

Using fear as a set-up.

set-up

Most people are afraid of dying because they don't know if they'll end up in heaven or hell. And to make it worse, they'll be completely alone.

punchline

Not me. Either place I go, I'll know plenty of people.

A punch line...
is created from the set-up

Using mortality to joke about

set-up

The conflict is, some people treat death as a disease to cure. If we eat fresh vegetables and avoid fried foods, we can beat death. Add regular exercise to that and the odds go way up. There is also the notion if we treat people right and give to the needy, we will be spared from dying.

Guess what? We can eat broccoli, run marathons and follow Mother Theresa's path and one day we all will die.

punchline

The conclusion – living healthy is the slowest way to die.

Set-ups
words
phrases
situations
...to joke about

Punch Lines
... are created from the set-up using -
word play
absurdity
distortion

Word Play

n multiple meaning of words

Wendy, "Mom and I were watching TV. The phone rang. Mom answered. She nodded a few times and hung up.

"'That was Aunt Maude's nursing home.' mom said. 'The nurse said Maude took a turn for the worse.'

"'A turn for the worse?' I said. 'What does that mean?'

"'She died.'

"'Oh,' I said. 'That is a turn for the worse. Did the nurse say exactly what happened?'

"'All she said was that Aunt Maude "expired."'

"'Expired?' I laughed. 'What is she, milk?'"

Absurdity

adj ridiculous, illogical, incongruous

Mark and **Tommy** were in hospice rooms next to each other. Tommy was known for his practical jokes. Mark was quiet. The men died within hours of each other.

Tommy's family waited in his room for the funeral home staff to pick up the body. The family sat for hours, but no one came.

Harry, Tommy's brother, called the funeral home. The director said Tommy was already in their care. Harry said there was a mistake. They were looking at his body.

The funeral director insisted he had the right body. It took 20 minutes to convince him that his staff had picked up the wrong guy.

Harry hung up and said, "Even when he's dead, Tommy's still playing practical jokes."

The family loved it.

Distortion

v to twist, stretch, exaggerate.

Roberta Long, "When I found out my dear friend Esther had terminal cancer, I immediately went to see her. When I asked Esther what she wanted to do with the time she had left, she said, 'travel.'

"I suggested Esther plan a trip. If she couldn't get a family member to go with her, I said I'd love to.

"Esther started worrying. She asked a bunch of 'what ifs.' 'What if I get sick?' 'What if I lose my medications?' 'What if I get lost?'

"I tried to reassure her. It didn't help. Finally, I interrupted, 'What's the worst that can happen?'

"Surprised, Esther said, 'I could die.'

"I smiled and said, 'Then pack your coffin.'

"Esther was stunned and stared for a long time. Finally she smiled. Then Esther burst out laughing and didn't stop for what seemed like an hour."

Some may find laughing at death irreverent, but it's vital to find humor in the things that scare us most.

WHY?

Humor is like faith. It pulls us out of fear – giving the hope of better days ahead.

hospice workers

2.

Hospice workers put in long hours.

They continually work in spite of emotional and physical exhaustion.

They are dedicated to helping people at the end of life.

They do it day after day, week after week.

Why they do it

Hospice aid,
"I help offer dignity to the patient who can no longer feed himself or perform the simplest bathroom skill. When you can no longer take care of yourself, you feel worthless. I give my patients worth."

Hospice nurse,
"When you work in a hospital, you can fix people's problems. In hospice there is nothing to fix – you make people comfortable. And that's essential."

Hospice nurse,
"I used to work in a hospital. The administration made me refer to my patients as a number. Here, our patients have a name."

Hospice social worker,
"I don't want someone to be alone in their scariest hour."

Nurse Joanna,
"To help a family is an honor and sacred ground. It's what gets me out of bed in the morning."

Nurse Phillip,
"What we do is hard, but important. When a loved one is dying, sometimes a family member is afraid to go in the room and say goodbye. We can help them overcome that fear. Later, they're always grateful to have had that last moment."

Nurse Patricia,
"I got a call from my 7-year-old son's teacher. She wanted to know what I did for a living.

"'I'm a hospice nurse,' I said. 'Why do you ask?'

"She laughed, 'Your son is telling his classmates you take care of dead people.'

"When my son got home I explained what I really do.

"'Oh,' he said. 'You help people get into heaven.'"

Nurse Marta,
"I have to laugh. It's the healthiest way to survive the doom and gloom of death."

Nurse Heidi,
"I can tell when I need to laugh, I'll cry at anything, even traffic jams. Thank goodness for our team meetings. One day we were talking about the new dress code. We decided to boycott and have our own dress code. From now on, we joked, nurses would be required to wear spandex and Wonderbras."

Nurses aid,
"You have to laugh with the family that misunderstood when I said we needed new bedding. The next day, the four sons carried in a new bed."

Nurse Sarah,
"Humor gives us a much needed break from the intensity of our job."

How they do it

Nurse Debbie,

"Hospice humor? You've got to be kidding! Death and dying? That's serious stuff. What could you laugh at in a hospice? But you learn to laugh.

"You laugh with a co-worker who complained about a foul odor and later found a dead mouse in her pocket – put there by a patient as a practical joke.

"You laugh at a teaching session demonstrating proper procedure for changing a roll of toilet paper.

"You learn laughter relieves pain like medication, but with far fewer side effects.

"You learn laughter adds life to the days of a dying patient.

"You learn the most deadly of all life-threatening conditions is the absence of laughter. Yet, this condition is curable, simply by learning to laugh."

“Humor gives us a newfound energy once death enters our lives.

“As we work with dying patients and their families, humor tumbles out in places we least expect. Laughing in those moments creates a powerful connection that embraces our joy for each other.

“There are funny moments at hospice. Many of those situations have nothing to do with death, they’re just funny things that happen or are said.

“We take every laugh we can get – knowing it helps us, the patient and family.

“The following stories remind us of those funny moments, making it a bit easier to let go and move on.”

– Charlene Shibel, Director
Hospice and Home Health
Olathe Medical Center

The hospice dietician,

"I told Ed, a diabetic patient, that he didn't have to be so strict with his diet. Ed was ecstatic. He ate everything and as much as he wanted.

"One day, Ed told me he was getting better.

"'The doctor said I might be able to go home,' he said. 'Maybe I ought to start watching what I eat again.'"

Hospice Nurse Jackie,

"I got pulled over for speeding. I told the policeman what I do for a living. He told me what fine work we do at hospice then let me off with just a warning.

"Two months later, I was pulled over again. When I told that policemen what I do, he said, 'You need to slow down so more people don't die.'

"And wrote me a ticket."

Ed, a distinguished 85-year-old man, was in hospice. When the nurse asked about his bowel movements, Ed wouldn't talk. Out of frustration, the nurse left a calendar in his room with a note that read, "Put all bowel movements on this calendar."

Two days later the nurse checked the calendar. She found a note from Ed, "I've never had a bowel movement on a calendar and I'm not about to start."

Hospice administrator,

"A patient, Gus, died. Marjorie had the responsibility of calling the family. The cell phone rang and rang. No one answered.

"Meanwhile, Nurse Lana heard a phone ring in a patient's room. She answered it and a voice said, 'Hi. This is hospice calling. We're sorry to inform you that Gus has passed away.'

"'I know, Marjorie,' Lana said. 'I'm standing right next to him.'"

The hospice team was having a meeting about Gary. He was ready to die, but couldn't let go. His family was ready to help him and so was the hospice staff. It was hard for everyone.

Just as the team was deciding their next move, a new receptionist came in.

"I'm sorry for interrupting," she said, "but I'm supposed to tell you that Gary just died."

The team all clapped and cheered. One nurse even stood and said,

"Way to go, Gary!"

The look on the receptionist's face was priceless.

Nurse David,

"I went to check on Lilly, one of my favorite patients.

"'And how are you doing today?' I asked.

"Lilly said, 'I'm ready to go upstairs.'

"'You'll be happy,' I told her. 'It's a wonderful place and you'll be free of pain.'

"'You think I'm talking about heaven?' Lilly said.

"'You're not?' I asked.

"'No,' Lilly laughed, 'I'm talking about the second floor. My sweaters are up there and I need them.'"

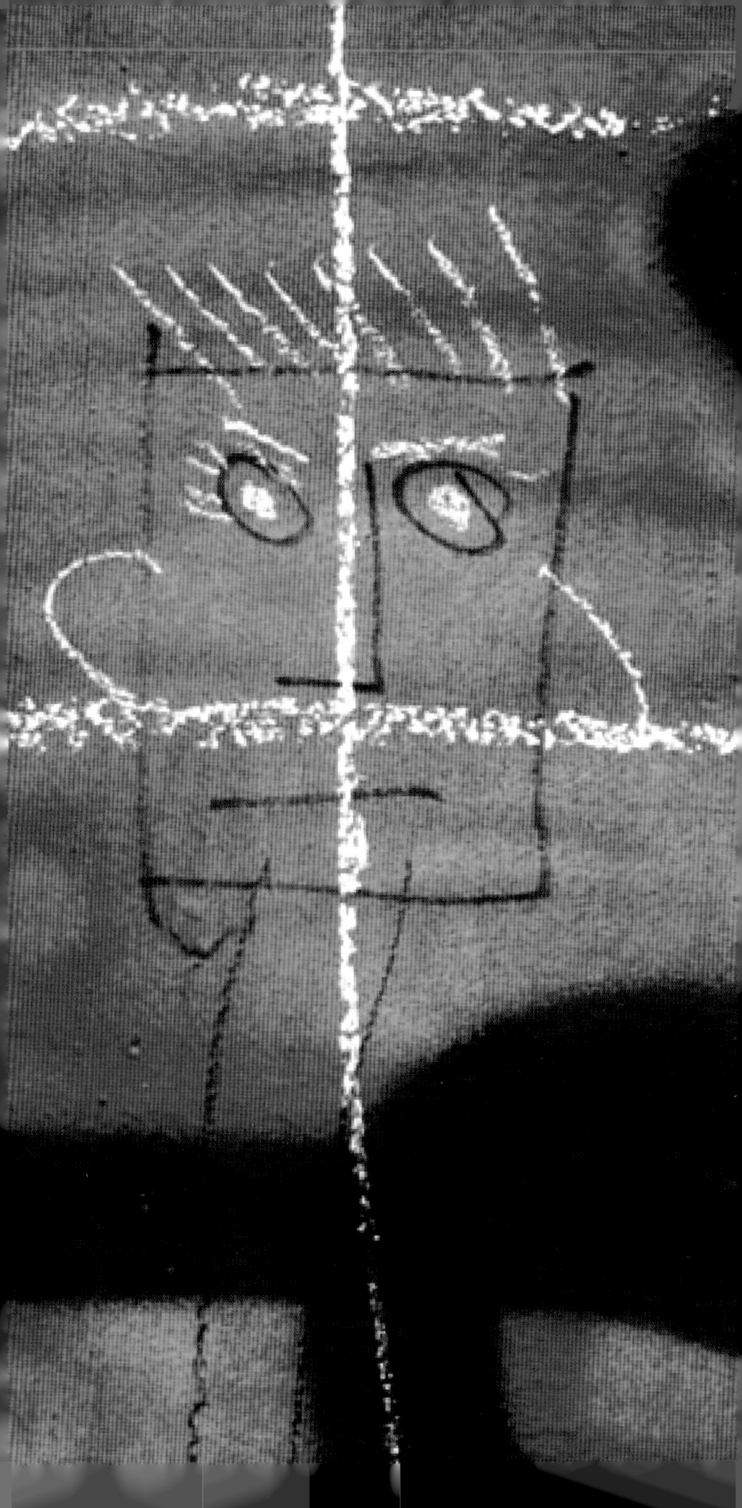

Betty,

"We were taking care of Ann, who was in her 90s. One day she had a worried look. I asked what was wrong.

"'Betty,' she said, 'don't people like me?'

"'Why?' I asked.

"'After my bath,' she said, 'I glanced at my chart. The aid had written "Patient SOB after bath."'

"'Ann,' I said, 'SOB means short of breath.'

"'Oh, good,' Ann said. 'I didn't think I was that bad.'"

Chaplain,

"The nurse told me Sally was awake even though she was totally unresponsive. She didn't move. She didn't open her eyes. She didn't speak.

"When I recited the Lord's Prayer, she didn't respond. I read the 23rd Psalm, no reaction. Finally, I started singing Amazing Grace. My voice isn't very good, but it didn't matter. Sally seemed to stir, so I sang the second verse even louder.

"When I started the third, Sally opened her eyes. She turned to me and said, 'Please … stop.'"

HELP
ME

Nurse,

"An 83-year-old man in hospice was delirious, constantly making up stories. One day while I was feeding him, his granddaughter called his cell phone. I answered.

"Grandpa grabbed the phone out of my hand and screamed, 'Help! Somebody call 911! They're holding me hostage!'

"He jumped, took off and soon I was chasing a naked 83-year-old man. It took a few nurses to catch him and lot of explaining to the granddaughter."

Nurse Irene,

"As we were checking in Norman, an 82 year-old man, he kept sticking his hand down my shirt. I'd casually move his hand and keep going.

"Then he put his hand up my skirt and grabbed my butt. Again, I moved his hand and continued.

"After I finally got Norman checked in, the unit manager came up.

"'I heard you did a fine job with your new patient,' he said.

"'I'm not sure if we got to second- or third-base,' I said. 'But I do know we are on a first-name basis.'"

Two nurses were discussing a patient who just died. The experienced nurse asked if anyone removed the patient's pain pump. The other nurse asked why. The nurse explained, "Because when the pump is out of medication, it beeps. And a beeping casket at the funeral would freak people out."

Chaplain,

"Arlene asked me to pray with her. We prayed for God to take away her pain. After only a few minutes, Arlene said she felt better.

"We prayed a while longer.

"'Oh, I feel so much better,' she said. 'I'd like to take a nap now. Thank you Chaplain.'

"When I walked outside, Arlene's mother asked if there was any improvement.

"'Yes,' I said beaming. 'We prayed. It really seemed to relieve her pain.'

"'I'm sure it did,' mom laughed. 'And the Demerol I gave her probably helped, too.'"

New nurse,

"Ninety-four-year-old Marge was miserable because she couldn't move around without great pain. We have some electric recliners that help people stand and sit. Unfortunately, Marge had to be put on a waiting list.

"One day, Marge was really hurting and said she just wanted to die. I asked if she needed anything.

"'Yes,' she said. 'You can get me a damn electric chair.'

"'We can't do that,' I said.

"'You mean I am not on the waiting list anymore?' Marge said.

"She was talking about the recliner. I thought she wanted to be electrocuted."

A hospice administrator,

"A bath aid was cleaning a 95-year-old man.

"'I know I don't have long to live,' the man said, 'but I have to know something. You've given baths to a lot of men, right?'

"'That's right,' she said. 'What do you want to know?'

"'Well,' he paused, 'I have to know something very important. How do I measure up?'

"The aid did her best not to look shocked. She smiled and gave him a thumbs up.

"That made his day. Maybe his life."

Nurse Billie,

"One of my first patients was an elderly gentleman. As he neared the end of his life he experienced periods of apnea, a temporary loss of breathing.

"One afternoon, the patient's son, daughter and wife were at his bedside. During one very long episode of apnea, his wife thought he had died. She threw herself across his body and started crying hysterically.

"The patient sat up and said, 'Woman, what in the hell do you think you're doing?'

"She straightened up, looked at him and said, 'Well … I was just practicing.'"

Jane,

"When we work in a patient's home, it's important to establish a genuine relationship. Once, I met a new patient, Miss Bessie. She was lying down, in her bedroom, in the dark.

"I said, 'Hi Miss Bessie, can you see me?'

"'I can't see nothing,' she said, 'I'm blind.'

"'Can you see shapes?' I asked.

"'I told you. I'm blind. I can't see nothing.'

"I grabbed her hand.

"'Well, in that case,' I said, 'I would like to introduce myself. My name is Jane. I'll be your hospice nurse. I'm very tall and skinny.'

"Miss Bessie started feeling my arm.

"'Girl,' she said, 'you're just a chunky little thing! I can tell you ain't tall and skinny.'

"From then on, anytime I walked in her house Miss Bessie would call out, 'Is that my chunky little thing?'"

Charles,

"My first job as a volunteer was to model for the new brochure. Since I'm in my 70s I looked like a patient. The photographer had me get in bed and wait while he went to get some equipment.

"A new nurse came on duty and saw me in bed.

"'Oh, I see we have a new patient. Do we need an enema?' she said.

"You wouldn't believe how fast I got out of that bed."

Rachel,

"I answer the phone at our center. The wrong numbers are the funniest."

"Good morning, Hospice."
"Oh no, I don't want to talk to you. (Click)"

"Good morning, Hospice."
"Hospice? I'm not ready for that yet. (Click)"

"Good morning, Hospice."
"I want to make an appointment with Dr. Burton."
"Of course. Are you a current hospice patient?"
"No. I just need a physical."
"You do know Dr. Burton's practice is limited to hospice care?"
"Does that mean she won't see me?"
"Are you in need of Hospice?"
"No ... I guess not. Darn it!"
(*And she hung up.*)

Chaplain,

"Vera, an 83-year-old patient, called me. She needed to talk about God. As I walked in her room, I said, 'Hi Vera. It's the Chaplain.'

"'I'm on the toilet,' she said, 'come on in here.'

"'Vera,' I said, 'I've never talked about the Lord in the bathroom.'

"'Well, pull up a chair Chaplain, because a holy wind is getting ready to blow.'

"And it did."

Nurse Paula,

"Late one night, 84-year-old Hank kept yelling, 'God, oh God!' You could hear it up and down the hall.

"From outside his door, I asked, 'Hank, are you okay?'

"'Is that you God?' he said.

"'Yes, it is,' I said. 'Now go to sleep.'

"And he did."

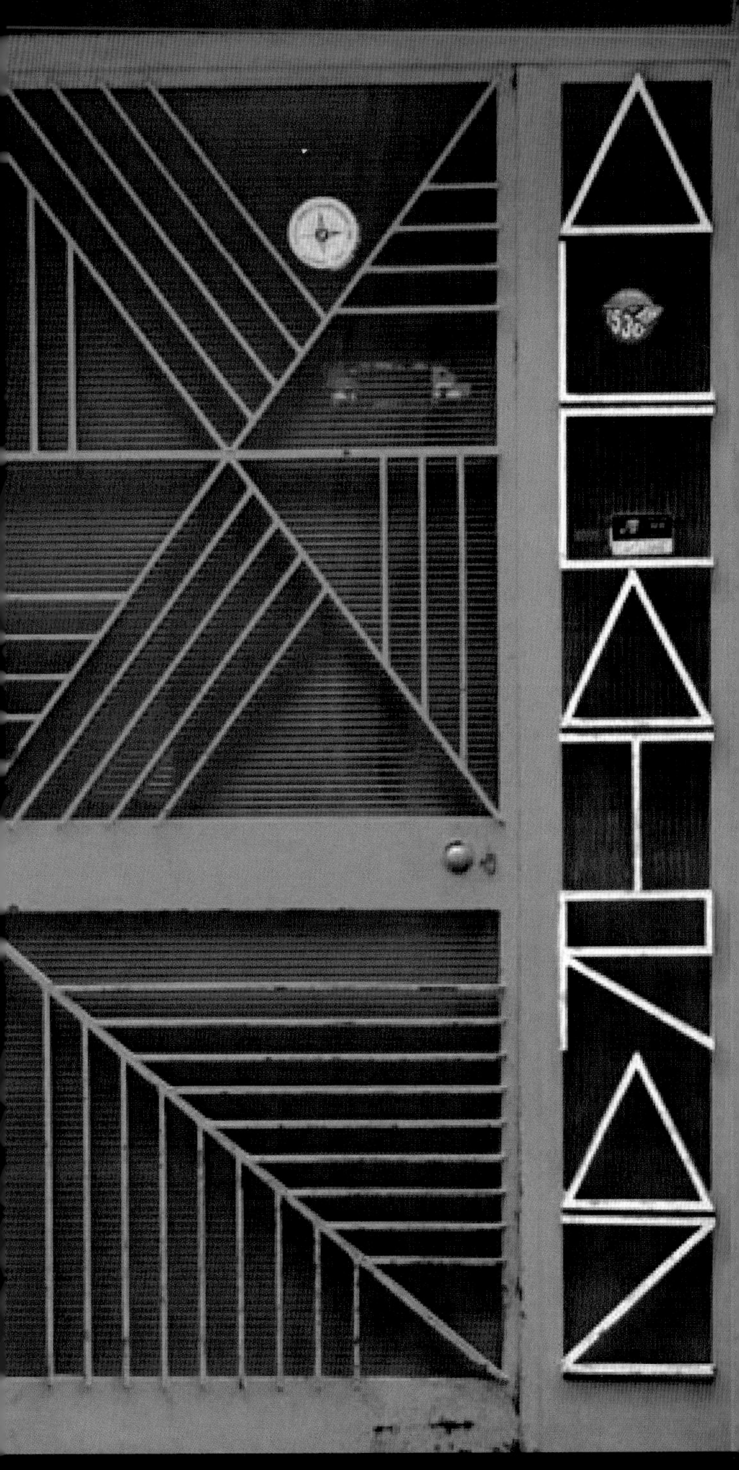

Hospice nurse,

"I was wearing scrubs when I picked up my daughter, Megan, from school. One of her friends asked, 'What does your mommy do?'

"'She's a nurse,' Megan said. 'And all of her patients die.'"

family

3

The humanity of humor

"If we don't understand death, we cannot understand life. The way we live is the way we die. We have to be careful to not exclusively put a spiritual realm around death, forgetting the dying person's humanity. That's why it's so important to know about my patients – because that's where the grief is.

"Grief is the life a person is giving up. While we embrace sadness and fear, we must never forget to laugh. Humor is also a part of our humanity.

"To laugh and experience joy in critical moments is crucial to our lives. We are not created to be sad sacks."

– *Sister Loretta Maguire*
St. Luke's Hospice

I did too

Julie, "Mom was in hospice and was becoming delirious. She constantly complained about hysterectomy pain.

"'Mom,' I told her, 'you never had a hysterectomy.'

"'I did too,' mom said, 'You wouldn't remember. It happened before you were born.'"

Sunday dinner

Kim, "Grandma Beatrice had hospice at her house. One Sunday afternoon, she started gasping for breath. We called the nurse. Then we called the family and told everyone not to wait for our traditional Sunday dinner, but come over right away.

"Everyone was in grandma's room watching as she struggled for breath. Then, suddenly, she stopped gasping and started breathing more easily.

"Grandma slowly looked around and said, 'If you all think I'm dying before dinner, you're nuts.'"

Inside only

Gwen, "When grandpa died, grandma asked all the grandkids to put something in grandpa's casket. Eight-year-old Kelly wanted to put a University of Georgia sticker in grandpa's casket. grandma wouldn't hear of it.

"She said, 'Your grandfather went to Georgia Tech, not the University of Georgia. Nothing to do with the University of Georgia will be inside his casket.'

"After the gravesite service, everyone was walking away as grandpa's casket was lowered in the ground. Little Kelly snuck back and put the Georgia sticker on the outside of grandpa's casket, honoring her grandma's request."

Fuzzy munchies

Rosy, "Aunt Lorraine and I were very close. When she went to hospice, I was there all the time. One night, she invited me to make myself something to eat, while she took a nap.

"In the kitchen, I made a sandwich and found some brownies. They were delicious. Later, Lorraine woke from her nap. I told her I felt funny. The room looked fuzzy and everything seemed to be moving in slow motion.

"Lorraine asked what I ate. When I mentioned the brownies, she laughed. She kept giggling, explaining the marijuana in the brownies helps relieve her pain.

"She continued to laugh till she had tears running down her face. It was the first time I'd seen her that happy in months."

An unfortunate time

Paulette, "Dad was 64 and didn't have long to live. As he lay in bed, Betty Carole, his high-school sweetheart walked in the room. She said hi to us then crawled in dad's bed.

"'George,' Betty Carole said, 'after all these years you finally got me where you want me – in bed with you.'

"'Betty Carole,' dad said, 'you got me at a most unfortunate time. The only thing that works in my pants is my pocket-knife.'"

Time to laugh

Carl, "Dad was very sick. One of his favorite possessions was a talking watch. The timepiece would call out the hour, on the hour. Dad loved it.

"One day I went to see him. When I walked in his house, dad looked like he was sleeping, so I didn't disturb him. Then I noticed his medication was sitting out. I went over to check on him, saw he was dead and immediately called 911.

"The paramedics asked if I wanted to try resuscitating dad. I declined. He was in no more pain.

"They covered him with a sheet and began their paperwork. One of the paramedics asked for the exact time of death. From under the sheet, dad's watch proclaimed, 'One o'clock pm!'

"The paramedics nearly jumped out of their shoes."

Table for 2

Darlene, "Aunt Jenny didn't have long to live, but she continued her radiation treatments hoping for a miracle. She had lost her hair and liked to wear stylish hats.

"One day, my dad was taking her for a radiation treatment. On the way, Jenny wanted something to eat. When they walked in the restaurant, dad looked around and said it was too crowded. She would miss her treatment.

"Jenny walked up to the hostess, 'I need lunch and I need it now.'

"'Ma'am,' the hostess said, 'we have a 30-minute wait.'

"Jenny pulled off her hat, 'I don't have much time.'

"They were seated immediately. The funny thing – Jenny was referring to her doctor's appointment, not how long she had to live."

What a pilot

Sue, "Our family has always had a good laugh, no matter the circumstances. My mother, Joan, died unexpectedly. She was 84.

"When the minister was preparing the eulogy, he asked if mom had any special nicknames. My husband, Don, said, 'Nothing we could repeat.'

"We went to the registrars office to get the death certificate. When the clerk asked if mom had a profession, again my husband joked, 'Oh yes, she was a pilot.' The registrar believed him and asked, 'What kind of planes?'

"'She didn't fly planes,' Don said, 'but you wouldn't believe the way she could fly that broom – everywhere and anywhere.'

"At the grave service, all of the family began to place a flower on mother's casket. As our daughter walked up, Don called out, 'Don't throw it into the crowd honey, that's next week.'

"He was refering to her wedding in seven days."

Highwaters

Nurse Patty, "When the family laughs at a lighter moment, it pulls them together.

"Thomas, an 88-year-old man, had grown frail. He weighed, maybe, 85 pounds, but kept wearing his old clothes.

"One time, Thomas sat in his wheelchair. I got out my stethoscope to check him. His pants were literally pulled up to his armpits. I stopped and laughed. He asked what was the matter.

"'Thomas,' I said, 'in all my years of nursing, I've never had to ask a patient to pull his pants down so I could check his heart.'

"The family had a huge laugh.

"Thomas' pants became a running joke. His last birthday card, from his daughter, showed an old man with his pants up to his chest."

Just trying to help

Bill, "I sat in a hospital room with my wife and her sister. Leone, their 95-year-old grandma, was dying. The nurse told us that right before someone dies they take a series of deep breaths. But Leone was breathing deeply for hours. The girls became emotionally and physically exhausted.

"Being a smart-ass I said, 'Leone, take your last breath. You're pissing us off.'

"The girls laughed. It did relieve the tension.

"Leone died a few minutes later. I don't know why. Maybe I pissed her off."

I’m not here

Grandpa died in his house. Our family was there. We joined hands and began praying. At this solemn moment, the phone rang.

Nobody stopped to answer. We continued to pray. The loud ring filled the house. On the ninth ring, the answering machine went off. It was grandpa’s voice, of course; it was his house.

We all heard grandpa say, “Hi. I’m not here right now. If you leave a message I’ll try to get back to you, but I’m not sure when that will be.”

Come in

Matthew, "Uncle Tim's 82-year-old girlfriend wanted to get baptized as she only had a month to live. He asked me to go with him.

"Tim knocked on his girlfriend's door.

"'Come in,' she said brightly.

"We walked in. I don't think she was expecting me. Uncle Tim's 82-year-old lady was in a red satin teddy, lying sideways on the bed, striking a Marilyn Monroe pose.

"That's something I'll never forget."

Funny things happen when family members die. The challenge is to recognize the humor and realize it's okay to laugh.

Dad did better

Judy, “When my dad moved to the hospice house I stayed with him most of the time. One night, my sister relieved me so I could get some sleep. I left around 10 at night. Four hours later, my sister called. She told me to come back immediately. Dad wasn’t doing very good. He died an hour later.

“After the funeral home took dad, we sat in silence. I started laughing. ‘What’s so funny?’ my sister asked.

“‘You know,’ I kept laughing, ‘dad did a lot better with me.’”

grief

4.

When someone you love dies or is dying, you get sad, even mad. Why shouldn't you? If there's a time to be emotional, that's it.

And that's healthy.

Grief only becomes unhealthy when it gets out of control. A snowball of sadness can turn into an avalanche of grief that will bury you alive.

Humorstopsthatmomentum, freeing you to move on with your own life.

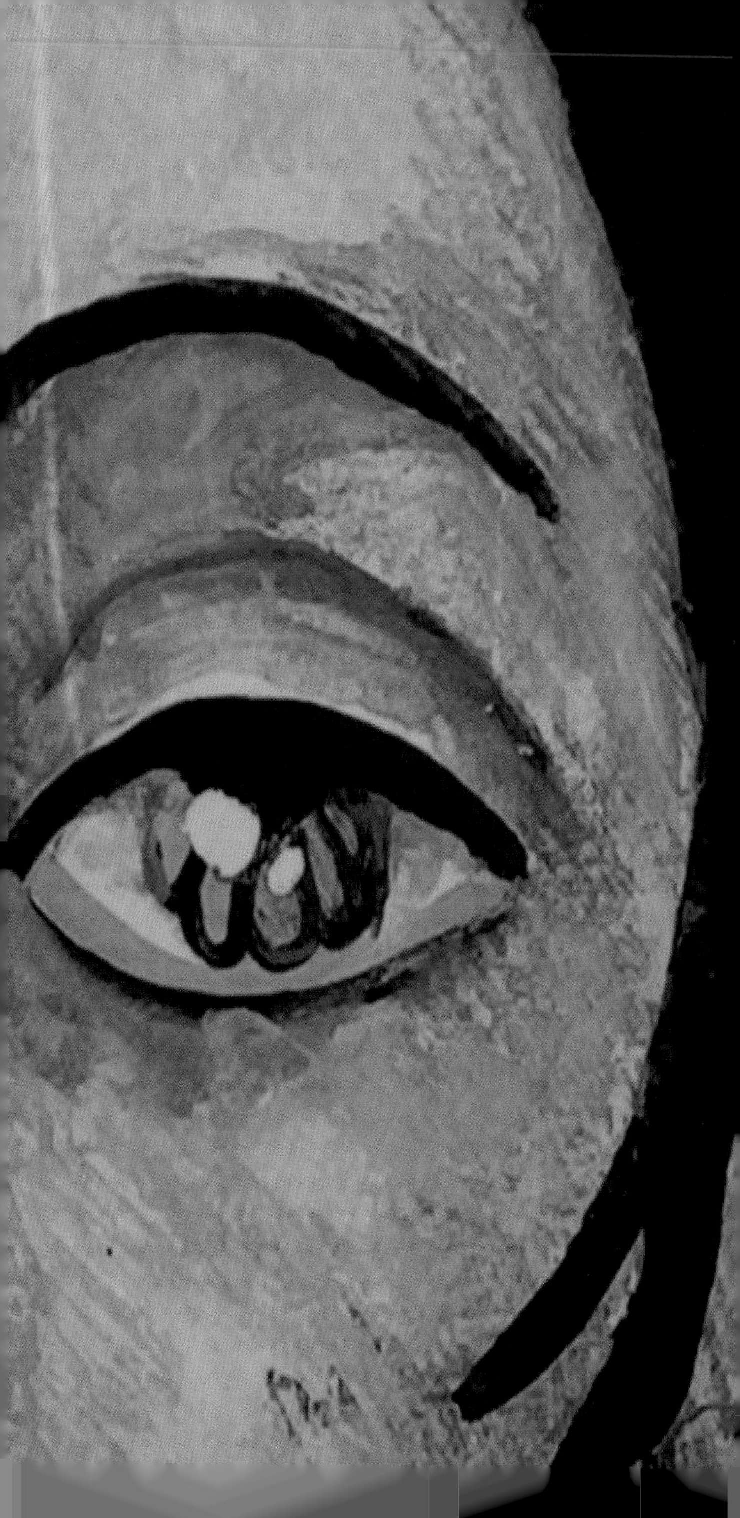

Taylor (12 years old)

"When grampa died, I was very sad. We had great times together. At his funeral, I remembered something funny.

"Every time grampa would get upset about anything, he would say, 'Dammit, Evelyn,' real quiet, under his breath.

"Grandma would always say, 'Just shush, Henry.'

"If grampa lost his glasses, stubbed his toe, when they ran out of milk – you could hear him all over the house, 'Dammit, Evelyn'

"Even weeks after the funeral, when I thought of grampa muttering, it made me smile.

Nancy,

"When I heard my Uncle Jack died, I was sad, then smiled. Every time I think of him, I remember being seven years old and playing the piano. When I hit certain notes, my dog would howl.

"Once, I made Jack watch as I tried to make the dog sing. I played and played, but the dog was quiet.

"Finally, after 20 minutes, my Uncle Jack stared howling. Then the dog jumped in."

S O L O

Chaplain Steve Smith,

"The deceased wrote her own eulogy and asked that 'Somewhere Over the Rainbow' be played at the conclusion. While reading this glowing eulogy, I noticed people giving each other puzzled looks. Apparently, the dearly departed wasn't quite as wonderful as she thought.

"At the conclusion of the speech I said, 'And this is how she wished to be remembered.'

"At that sensitive moment, 'Somewhere Over the Rainbow' from 'The Wizard of Oz' was supposed to play. But someone pressed the wrong button. 'Ding-Dong, the Witch is Dead' came over the sound system instead."

Lori

"My cousin's 13-year-old son, Danny, was killed while roller-blading. The family met at my cousin's house and all began crying and talking. Dad and I began reminiscing what a wonderful person Danny was.

"'Hey,' I said, 'I wonder if there are large displays in heaven, like in airports, that show daily arrivals? Loved ones who've died before would say, "Look who's coming today. Let's go meet them!"'

"At this thought, my father and I began to laugh. Granted, this isn't a knee-slapper, but the thought of a 'Giant Concourse in the Sky' made it easier to deal with the loss of a wonderful young man."

Reverend Emmanuel Cleaver, "When my mother died it was the deepest funk I had ever been in. I'd never experienced that kind of depression. I almost gave up the ministry.

"A pastor friend phoned. He offered condolences, and then started joking with me. Soon I was laughing. I couldn't believe it. I thought I'd never laugh again. Proverbs was right, 'A merry heart doeth good like medicine.'

"People ask me how long to mourn for a lost loved one. I quote Psalms 30:5: 'Weeping may tarry the night, but joy comes with the morning.' I believe in that passage. A single day is all people should grieve. Like darkness gives way to light, misery must give way to joy.

"I'm not the only one who believes this. I sat with Bill Cosby after his son, Ennis, was killed. Bill was making everybody in the room laugh — doing an impression of his minister.

"Bill later told me, 'It was time to get on with enjoying life. That's what my son would want me to do.'"

Research has found that focusing only on negative emotion lengthens the grieving period. But people who laugh while mourning move on more quickly.

Julia,

"Katie, my beloved cocker spaniel, died after 15 years. I had her cremated and keep the ashes in my living room.

"When mom died we had her cremated, as well. After the service, my best friend Tonya asked, 'Where are you going to put your mom?'

"'In the living room,' I said, 'next to Katie. That way I can have both my bitches together.'"

Rabbi Alan Cohen,

"When I conduct a funeral, I choose my words carefully to evoke a pleasant memory of the departed — not to be a comedian. People in attendance, especially the family, appreciate those funny memories.

"One man was late his entire life. During his eulogy I said, 'This day, he was finally on time.'

"At another service, I said of a woman, 'She would never, ever let me get the last word. Today, I will.'"

Jill,

"As mom was dying she told me and my two sisters, 'Do not take out my dentures. No matter what.'

"Shortly after, mom went into a coma. We never left her side. Even though she was unconscious, her mouth kept moving – clicking her dentures.

"After hours of the annoying sound, my youngest sister couldn't take it any longer. She said, 'I'm taking those dentures out.'

"She got up, walked over and slipped her fingers in mom's mouth. Mom bit down so hard my sister couldn't get her fingers out. What made us laugh was that mom was still unconscious."

final funnies

HEY
HEY

Some people are funny right up to their final breath. Do they do it for themselves or for their grieving loved ones?

Maybe both.

Either way, we laugh.

What a great memory!

Herman,

"I may be 101 years old, but I got news for you, I ain't beating death. Far as I can recollect, the death rate is, and will always be 100%. There ain't no cure and no doctor can fix it.

"So what am I going to do about it? Go have some strawberry ice cream and a snickerdoodle.

"How the hell do you think I made it this long?"

BAD
BOY
STAL

Susan,

"My husband, Bob, was dying. Our family stood around his bed. Three times Bob sat up, reached for the ceiling, gasped, then fell back on the bed and grabbed my hand.

"On the fourth time, he grabbed my boob.

"Our son said, 'Dad ain't dead yet!'"

Funeral director,

"While a woman was pre-planning her funeral, she nonchalantly told me she was flat-chested and to make sure she was facing the right way in her casket.

"A month later she died. When I began preparing her for the funeral, I started laughing. Written on her chest in magic marker was, 'This side up.'"

Jim Fussell's dad, Jerome, was an expert on proper grammar. He worked as an editor for Webster Dictionaries.

Jim, "Dad was on his deathbed, with just a few hours left. My sister, Nancy, ran in the room with her husband.

"'Daddy, I am so sorry John and me didn't get here sooner. What can we do?'

"Dad motioned with his frail hand, calling her closer. With Nancy's ear next to his lips, dad whispered, 'John and I.'

"What a great way to remember him."

A**rt Buchwald** was a Pulitzer Prize winner. When his kidneys failed he refused dialysis and chose hospice.

When asked by a reporter what dying was like he said, “Dying isn’t hard. Getting paid by Medicare is.”

Bally
BOW AND
1UP
2 2 6 3 0
3UP
0 0 0 0 0
AN PLAY

Pedro,

"My 101-year-old grandma had an incredible sense of humor. She had to, surviving Castro's Cuba.

"When grandma met with the funeral director to select her plan, she said, 'Give me the simplest casket you have. Then mount a rearview mirror on it.'

"'That's a first,' the director laughed.

"'I've had a wonderful life,' she said. 'While I'm lying there, I want to look back on it.'"

Legendary comedian Bob Hope proved to be funny right up to the end. With not long to live, his wife, Dolores, asked him where he would like to be buried.

Bob said, "Surprise me."

2

Author Oscar Wilde was destitute and living in a cheap boarding house when he found himself on his deathbed. His last words were:

"This wallpaper will be the death of me – one of us will have to go."

Nurse Patty,

"I asked a 102-year-old woman if she was afraid to die.

"She said, 'No, I'm ready to go.'

"'Is something stopping you?' I said. 'You know you'll probably meet your late husband.'

"'That's what's stopping me,' she said."

Polly,

"When my mother visited her dying brother she told him, 'I don't like funerals. So, I just want you to know, I won't be coming to yours.'

"'That's okay,' he said, 'I wouldn't be able to talk to you anyway.'"

...closing comments

"Life is hard."

"Death is harder."

"Grief may be the worst feeling we ever endure. I would never suggest to just laugh, and not feel the deep sadness of loss.

"I would though, recommend to laugh when something funny does happen because it stops the momentum of sadness. Humor makes the path to healing easier.

"Laughing at death is like owning a car. A car, like us, will one day, quit running. But we must never stop enjoying the ride.

"Sometimes the journey is bumpy, causing numerous stops. Other times it's fun and easy. Either way, we keep driving.

"When we find humor and laugh at death, it doesn't mean we're irreverent. It simply means we are finding a way to get through life's toughest road by enjoying the funny detours."

Momento mori!
David

45
50
30
60
70
mph
km
E
F

- Keynote speaking
- Workshops
- Humor coaching
- Books
- Laugh store

Questions?

Please visit
naster.com

Winner of the
2007 Humor Book Award
AATH
(Association of Applied Therapeutic Humor)

Winner of the

2008 Humor Book Award

AATH

(Association of Applied Therapeutic Humor)